Sad Fred

by Alexandra Anderson
illustrated by Rachel Barber

Practice Decodable 21

Mc Graw Hill Education

Bothell, WA • Chicago, IL • Columbus, OH • New York, NY

MHEonline.com

Send all inquiries to:
McGraw-Hill Education
8787 Orion Place
Columbus, OH 43240

ISBN: 978-0-02-144745-9
MHID: 0-02-144745-4

Printed in China.

8 9 10 11 12 DSS 27 26 25 24 23

When Fred is sad, he gets his drums.

Sad Fred raps his drums.

Rap, rap, rap.

Sad Fred taps his drums.
TAP! TAP! TAP!

Sad Fred slams his drums.

BAM! BAM! BAM!

When Fred is not sad, he stops.

When Fred is not sad, I am glad.